THE OLD, THE MAD AND THE WOBBLY

Also by Heather Cook

Evie's Diary
Paws for Thought
From Sidcup with Purrs

THE OLD, THE MAD AND THE WOBBLY

All cats are special,
but some are more special than others

HEATHER COOK

PHOTOGRAPHS BY ROGER COOK

Matador
9 Priory Business Park,
Wistow Road, Kibworth Beauchamp,
Leicestershire. LE8 0RX
Tel: 0116 279 2299
Email: books@troubador.co.uk
Web: www.troubador.co.uk/matador
Twitter: @matadorbooks

ISBN 978 1784624 903

British Library Cataloguing in Publication Data.
A catalogue record for this book is available from the British Library.

Typeset in 12pt Book Antiqua by Troubador Publishing Ltd, Leicester, UK
Printed and bound in the UK by TJ International, Padstow, Cornwall

Matador is an imprint of Troubador Publishing Ltd

For all my friends, human and feline

Lord Wispy

INTRODUCTION

This is a book about cats that are special. They're all special, I hear you cry and of course this is true. It's just that some cats are more special than others and over the years a considerable number of "special" cats have taken up residence at Tresta Towers. For nearly 30 years I was the homing officer for Woking Branch of Cats Protection and this afforded me an endless supply of cats that could variously be described as "past their sell-by date", "off-the-wall" or "damaged". Some of these have presented me with significant challenges, but there is no such thing as a bad cat. This implies that the creature is deliberately behaving in a way that conflicts with human standards, whereas I believe that animals are much more straightforward, reacting to outside stimuli, favourable or unfavourable, in order to survive.

In recent years I have surrounded myself with special cats to the point where I would probably struggle to cope with a perfectly normal cat, even assuming there might somewhere be such a creature. So what are the attractions of sharing your life with these feline "misfits"?

A kitten is a kitten, but each mature cat is unique. Shaped by experience – good and bad; a survivor, whether it has wrestled with the dark forces of nature or nothing more demanding than securing the most comfortable billet on the sofa. Older cats are not afraid to be themselves – not that there's ever any real danger of cats worrying what anybody thinks. Mature cats have had years to grow into their ears and even if their ears don't hear too well, those cats still have plenty to say.

Madness happens: in cats as in people. It can take the form of harmless eccentricity, dementia or out and out psychosis. In cats it can be a rather attractive quality, only necessitating the wearing of protective clothing in extreme cases. Think of kittens racing round a room at head height, their tails like loo brushes and their ears like helicopter blades. See what I mean? They start off bonkers and it can only get worse.

Like madness, wobbliness can occur at any age. I should explain that "wobbliness" is a non-scientific term, used here to cover a host of disabilities and missing components. Some cats are born wobbly, some achieve wobbliness and some have wobbliness thrust upon them by illness or accident.

Of course these categories overlap and mingle, like the glorious autumn colours in a tortoiseshell cat's coat. This book tells the tale of some of the special cats that have shared and continue to share my life and if after reading about them a few readers decide that an older or disabled cat might fit into their lives rather snugly, that would make this silly old catwoman extremely happy.

CHAPTER ONE

A Furry Inheritance – Where There's A Will, There's A Cat

Before I embarked on true life cat rescue, I used to think that every cat or kitten needing a home had been placed in that unfortunate position because of human cruelty or neglect. This theory was disproved at an early stage as I was brought face to face with the impact of human misfortunes on much-loved pets. This section of the book features those cats that have come into my life after their loving owners have either died or been forced to leave their homes, leaving behind a bewildered and lonely companion.

Nothing could have prepared me for the awfulness of lifting a warm and purring elderly cat from its owner's lap and whisking it away. What can you say that doesn't sound unduly chirpy and false? How can you reassure a sobbing octogenarian that you will find a loving home for their much-loved and quite possibly only companion of many years standing? And how can you possibly comfort the panic-stricken cat that is yowling, vomiting and piddling on the back seat of your car as you whisk through the darkened streets, knowing that it will never see its home again and instead will be installed in a clean and functional cat pen for an indefinite period of time?

Sometimes the owner would welcome news of their

much-loved pet; sometimes – and I do understand this – they would choose to draw a line under things, but I'm sure there wouldn't have been a day when they didn't think about their old friend. Various elderly acquaintances have frequently told me that the worst thing about having to go into a care home wasn't parting with the furniture they had treasured for sixty years, or the garden full of scented roses, or even, in one case, some ancient cow bells inherited from before The Flood. It was saying "goodbye" to their furry friend.

I would like to say that the cats in question were equally heart-broken, but this wouldn't be true and those of you who have faced up to the masochistic nature of cat worship would never believe me if I said they were. The general pattern of events would be that I would arrive home with a shivering, deeply unhappy cat, remove more pee, poo and vomit than you would ever think could issue forth from such a skinny old bag of bones, and settle it into a cat pen, confident in the knowledge that it would yowl all night.

In the morning, I would totter outside with a tray loaded with irresistible goodies and find the cat shivering on an outside ledge, having vowed to never lie in the warm bed so lovingly provided. Often I would bring a carload of possessions from the cat's previous home – possessions it would stare at as if they had lately come from Mars; sometimes the cat would come with nothing more than a barely recognisable toy mouse, having resolutely refused to sleep anywhere other than on its owner's bed.

It goes without saying that the food would remain untouched and often the only response I could elicit would be a hiss and a low growl. Fast forward a few days, by which time my reluctant lodger would have realised that she was safe and could be warm if only she could find it in her heart to do the sensible thing and make use of the cosy bed. Soon there would be signs of secret eating and instead of hisses and growls I would be greeted with encouraging if muted "chirrups".

A general truth was that the cat would always be full of surprises. If the owner said that Fluffy would only eat fish, you could put money on Fluffy looking at a plate of boiled cod as if you had presented her with a lump of fox poo. If the owner insisted on sending Fluffy off with her "favourite" teddy because the two were inseparable, you could confidently look forward to finding Teddy headfirst in Fluffy's water bowl by the next morning.

I was particularly wary whenever I was told that the cat loved being groomed after a tentative brushing of Gnasher's knotted coat had me sending out for sandwiches from a crowded Accident and Emergency Department. It wasn't Gnasher's fault, of course – nothing ever was. Just the faintest sign of remorse would have made me feel better about things, but Gnasher's tail-swishing insistence that he was the wronged party was slightly hurtful.

Sadly, many animals belonging to very elderly people who are struggling to look after themselves, never mind a pet, are themselves elderly and in need of veterinary treatment. Typically, the annual booster jabs which would necessitate a visit to the vet and a health check would have lapsed. The updating of inoculations is easily accomplished, but often various health conditions which had remained undiagnosed – sometimes for years – would require more radical intervention.

This would often give rise to a phenomenon known in cat rescue circles as the reverse ageing process. You would bring a poor old cat into care, have a blood test or two taken, and after a few weeks of appropriate medication – frequently to manage an overactive thyroid – the recently acquired listless wreck would be knocking seven bells out of a catnip mouse and swinging from its scratching post.

Over the years I have had the privilege of meeting a great number of feline characters and the following pages are a tribute to some of the sparkiest old sausages you could ever wish to meet. If they had been human they would almost certainly have been unbearable!

Amber

I hadn't been involved in cat rescue for long when I had a phone call about a stray cat stealing bird food and generally making herself unpopular. Enquiries had been made and no owner traced, so I dragged my trusty cat trap from the depths of the garage and set off, endeavouring to remember how to negotiate a roundabout, overcome as I very nearly was by the overpowering aroma of pilchard – the tried and tested bait for luring wild and deeply suspicious felines into a trap.

Mercifully the lady concerned was more than happy to leave me to it. There is nothing worse in this situation than the well-meaning person who hovers helpfully at your elbow, talking in a stage whisper and tripping over the trap so that it goes off with a resounding crash, ensuring that the skulking shadow that might have been the feral in question will disappear for at least a week. And why some people would feel the need to fling half a chicken and a side of salmon at a cat just before the appointed trapping time, I never did fathom, but in this case I couldn't fault the woman other than to wish she'd let me get off the doorstep before slamming the door and turning all the lights out.

I placed the pilchard in the trap and retreated into the shadows. Soon, a small black cat appeared and circled round the trap, poking a paw through the wire in a doomed attempt to hook out some fish. I held my breath as she placed a dainty black paw in the entrance of the trap. Trapping, like so many activities in life, is characterised by long periods of boredom punctuated by brief spells of heart-stopping panic, and this was no exception.

The cat toyed with my emotions repeatedly, popping in and out and even sitting inside the trap to have a good wash. Eventually, just as I was wondering if I would ever know what it was like to be warm and comfortable again, she went right to the end of the trap, stood on the pressure pad and the door slammed shut. I staggered forward with a blanket and threw it over the trap to quieten the poor creature down and hauled the whole lot onto the back seat of the long-suffering and perpetually pilchard-scented car.

I released the cat into the cattery-style cat pen and was pleased to see that she didn't hurtle into the furthest corner, adopting a more measured approach and finding the time and composure to spit at me as she sauntered towards the cosy sleeping quarters. I wasn't absolutely sure that the cat was female, but she looked "girlie" and there were no obvious spherical features at the rear end. I decided to call her "Amber" because her eyes were – yes, you've got it – a most striking and glowing amber.

At this early stage in my cat rescuing career, I still laboured under the misapprehension that every cat could be tamed if enough love was thrown at it. As time went on, I had dealings with many true ferals – cats that were far wilder than your average fox – that wanted nothing more than to keep as much distance between them and the human race as possible. Tiny kittens could usually be brought on and homed, and domestic cats that had run wild could often be rehabilitated, but I came to realise that the kindest way of helping adult, out-and-out ferals was generally to trap them, neuter or spay them and return them to live their lives as wild animals. Sometimes it made sense to relocate them to a safer area and we achieved some notable successes in this respect when a resident lunatic was threatening to shoot or poison them at their original location.

Amber turned out not to be a true feral, although she could give a convincing impression of one if called upon to do so and always managed to behave like a wild thing whenever a prospective owner arrived to see her. After a while I was beginning to feel quite desperate as no cat should spend too long in a pen, even a fairly roomy one, so one day I opened the door and let her out. She settled quite happily as a garden cat, but as summer slipped into autumn Amber decided that she needed to sort out a more satisfactory arrangement and targeted my next door neighbour – the lovely Clauda, who cooked like a dream. In fact, the aromas that issued forth from her kitchen were so tantalising that I'm surprised half the street hadn't moved in with her.

Amber lived happily there for years before a shadow loomed over her sunny existence. Clauda and I were sharing a bottle of wine in the garden one golden September evening when she suddenly told me that she was terminally ill and asked me to promise that I would look after Amber when she'd gone. I was devastated and could think of nothing remotely sensible to say other than to gibber about her husband keeping the cat; he would, wouldn't he?

She smiled and said in tones devoid of resentment that Gerry would be all over the place when she died and she knew that he would never cope with Amber. Of course I promised – not because I really believed her, but because I was anxious to allay her concerns.

A few months later, my dear friend passed away at home with her husband holding her hand. Amber was under the bed and the second that her owner's pulse stopped, the cat dashed out of the bedroom, never to return. Two weeks passed by before Gerry came to my door and said that Amber had been sick on the kitchen floor and he couldn't possibly deal with this. I was reluctant to take Amber into my home because she had been quite feisty with some of my old cats and also I thought it would be very difficult for her to settle so close to her old home.

I decided that a comfortable kennel in my garden would be the best solution and did my best to convince Amber of the advantages. She looked at me strangely, her lip hooked up on a prominent canine tooth.

A few days later I was sitting in the lounge thumbing through a magazine when I vaguely noticed that there was a black cat asleep on the armchair by the window. This was odd, because I'd just seen my black cat stuffing its face in the kitchen.

It was Amber, who had obviously made up her mind that she was going to join the home team and if I thought she was going to live in some outhouse – however luxuriously appointed –I'd got another think coming. From that moment on, Amber never strayed from the house or the back garden. At no time did I ever see her on the doorstep of her old home and when Gerry popped in, she turned her back on him. Only once, when she was in the garden helping me with some planting, did she suddenly turn round when Gerry's side gate opened, then shook her head and turned back to her gardening duties. I think for a moment she must have thought it was Clauda coming home, but dismissed the thought with a shake of the head.

Amber was with me for many years and asserted her authority with a deft jab of her greying left paw. As the other cats lurched into the kitchen at mealtimes, she would poke them and skitter away as if consumed with mirth. For months after she went to the Great Dirt Tray in the sky, the others would peer round doorways and rummage in impossibly small boxes, unable to accept that this tiny cat with the towering presence had finally left us.

Count Lucio

Have you ever suffered a loss of confidence with a professional person? I'm not talking about vets, who have been generally wonderful – compassionate, skilful and totally committed to easing suffering and saving life – but about solicitors, who with a few notable exceptions have been a resounding disappointment in my experience.

Disappointment is one thing, but when the wellbeing of a defenceless animal is involved, a dilatory approach to resolving matters is the last thing that's needed. This was the situation when an elderly couple of my acquaintance passed away within weeks of each other, leaving explicit instructions in their Will that any cats owned by them at the time of their death were to come to me. This arrangement had been agreed between us some years previously.

I had lived in the same house for thirty years at the time of their death, but their solicitor failed to contact me, later claiming that she thought she had spoken to me, but must have been mistaken. I only heard about Count Lucio's plight when a colleague from the local Cats Protection Branch mentioned it during a fascinating discussion about flea and worm treatments. The address rang a bell and I was soon the happy, if slightly surprised, owner of an extremely large black cat.

The novelty of having what at first appeared to be a perfectly normal cat in the household threw me into a state of near panic, familiar as I was with missing limbs, dementia and wobbliness, but we all settled down happily together. Lucio was a gentle giant, a handsome boy with a commanding presence; not over-gifted, perhaps, but who wants a bright cat?

He had only been with us for around three months when he disappeared. If you have ever lost a black cat, you will be aware of the difficulties. One woman, obviously a frustrated comedian, suggested that as black cats were so common, couldn't I just get another one? I shall not record my reply, but should an accident befall that person, I would not be inconsolable.

After several miserable days, my next door neighbour rushed round to tell me that a large black cat had just crossed her back garden and was heading towards our fence. We waited in vain for the familiar, panther-like shape to manifest itself and eventually found him huddled against our neighbour's fence in a state of collapse.

The vet examined our hero for signs of injury and concluded that he could be dehydrated and stressed and we would do well to see how things looked in the morning. Unfortunately, the morning brought us a cat resembling an over-ripe banana. Lucio's skin was an alarming yellow and his eyes and lips almost glowed. A diagnosis of pancreatitis did little to cheer us up and certainly did nothing for Lucio, who looked about as miserable as a cat could look without actually bursting into tears.

He was an in-patient for over a week, during which time my husband, generally known as Poor Roger, and I were frequent visitors. We took in a succession of irresistible goodies, which Lucio actually found all too easy to resist, skulking behind his dirt tray with his large ears at half-mast.

The vet suggested a referral to a specialist as Lucio's condition was failing to respond to the supportive treatment he was having, so we soon found ourselves speeding down the M25 with our droopy banana flopping about and moaning on the back seat. At this time I was awaiting a date for a hip replacement on the NHS; I didn't exactly begrudge Lucio his private medical care, but one or two less than charitable thoughts did spring to mind when the old joints were particularly creaky.

In the waiting room we were surrounded by pedigree cats and dogs, but Lucio more than held his own, gazing around with an expression that somehow combined an aristocratic loftiness with a need for sympathy. Once we were admitted to the inner sanctum, it took precisely ten seconds for him to charm the young lady consultant as he flung himself into her arms and gazed into her face, leaving Poor Roger and I to splutter incoherently about him not moving for days and seeming close to death.

After parting with over £2000 and spending several more hours on the M25, Lucio was finally well enough to come home. We installed him in our bedroom for a while to convalesce and organised our lives around his drug regime as animal people do. Shopping trips focussed on finding tasty things to tempt his jaded appetite and we had to restrain ourselves from behaving extremely badly if another shopper showed signs of clearing the shelf of Lucio's latest favourite. A good day was one when the patient condescended to clear his plate; a day of uneaten goodies would render us suicidal.

It was around this time that he became known as "Count Lucio" and this had much to do with his dominating presence on our bed. After a good night's sleep, the sight of a handsome black cat sprawled across a red cover might be a heartwarming thing. At midnight, when you're struggling to get to sleep under that same red cover it is the stuff of nightmares.

To everybody's relief, Count Lucio gradually returned to rude health and is with us still – a handsome and bulky figure, with more charm than is good for him and a brain the size of a shrivelled pea.

Whizzy

The woman on the end of the phone had been rendered incoherent by emotion and by the time I'd managed to grasp the import of her message, I was almost in the same boat.

'Dead! My friend was found dead! The neighbours hadn't seen her for a few days and phoned the Police. She'd always kept herself to herself and none of them had a key. I've got one, but they wouldn't have known that.'

Fortunately, I resisted the temptation to ask why she was telling me and gradually dredged up some blurred memory of promising to take somebody's cat if anything should befall them. Well, something obviously had befallen this poor woman, but before shuffling off this mortal coil she had had the foresight to pen a note with my name and number on and the word "cat" in a shaky hand. In fact, "cat" looked much more like "hat", but confronted by a wailing cat I couldn't blame the Police for interpreting it as they did.

I remembered now. Three-legged Vicky had been in my rescue pens and I had homed her with a delightful person who had seemed as fit as a flea at the time. I had taken Vicky to her new home, congratulating myself on finding a wonderful "forever" home for this sweet white and black girl. As I headed for the door, the new owner asked if I would promise to have the cat if something should happen because she had no relatives or friends who could take Vicky on. It was important for Vicky to live in a safe area because she had already lost one leg in an argument with a car and I lived in a quiet cul de sac. I agreed without a second thought and promptly buried the conversation in the darkest recesses of what passes for a brain.

It wasn't an ideal time to be taking on another cat. My dear old mother had just passed away and there was the inevitable sorting out to deal with; we also had twelve cats already – most of which could be termed "special". Still, a promise is a promise and I knew that Vicky needed to come to us. Poor Roger was less than enthusiastic when I mentioned this development as he returned from a happy hour of fountain poking in the darker recesses of the garden.

'However many more of these cats have you agreed to take?' he asked. 'No doubt you'll be bringing a carload of prisoners home one of these days!'

This last remark was a rather spiteful reference to the sweet boys that I visit at a local prison. Although I was disappointed by Poor Roger's reaction, I had a sneaking feeling that right was on his side. It would therefore be a mistake to engage in discussion on the subject and I adopted a lofty "never apologise, never explain" strategy which has served me in good stead over the years.

'I haven't got time to debate the matter,' I replied. 'I need to go and collect this poor bereaved cat. Perhaps you could get the kitten pen ready while I'm out – only if you've got time, of course.'

When I collected the cat I was informed by the neighbour that she was now called "Whisky" because her late owner had thought it a more appropriate name. This was obviously the least of the cat's worries, but I did feel that it had a rather masculine ring to it and resolved to hit upon something a trifle more feminine in due course.

Back home, all was in readiness for our new arrival and – predictably – Poor Roger was besotted with her as soon as he saw her. We have always started new cats off in a large kitten pen, which gives them the opportunity of observing their environment and the other residents from a safe refuge. The pen is large enough to accommodate a cosy bed, a dirt tray, food and water bowls and as well as providing a refuge it minimises the possibility of escapes. Once installed in her cage, Whisky made good use of the facilities, had a spirited spit at the cats peering in at her, then slept for hours.

As the days passed, it became pretty obvious that Whisky hated the other cats. We didn't require the services of a behavioural expert to tell us this; the way she lunged at the wire every time Stumpy Malone got within two feet of her tended to give the game away. After three weeks we opened the patio door and watched anxiously as she picked her way across the grass. At least we knew that she wouldn't be able to get over the six foot fence at the bottom with only one hind leg to propel her.

Five minutes later she was on the top of the six foot fence and only Poor Roger's timely and desperate intervention stopped her from leaping off into the woods behind the bungalow.

We decided to keep her indoors for a further three weeks to settle her down, but even after that she frightened us out of our wits by flying about all over the place. We regularly had reports from worried neighbours, who had found this poor three-legged cat in their back gardens and thought she wouldn't be able to get out. We would rush round to see the object of their concern hopping along the top of the fence without a care in the world.

The turning point for Whisky and for us came one sunny afternoon when we were all in the back garden. Whisky was sitting by the corner of the garage and on the other side of the garden a fat grey squirrel was pottering in the border. Whisky was watching him keenly, but we knew that she would never be quick enough to catch him. One minute later, after a lightning sprint across the grass, Whisky emerged with the squirrel clamped between her jaws, gave him a practised shake and flung his corpse down in front of us.

From that moment, our new girl assumed a more confident persona. She no longer retreated from the other cats, but asserted her authority with a quick jab whenever anyone invaded her personal space and no longer felt the need to rush half way across Surrey whenever we let her out, frightening us to death, because she knew that Tresta Towers was where she belonged. And we knew that she was no longer "Whisky", but a much more cheerful and cheeky girl called "Whizzy".

Miss Poppet

Isn't it just when you're relaxing and thinking all's right with the world that the double whammy comes? In this instance I was having lunch with a friend and we had reached that cosy point in the proceedings where I felt I could easily postpone the afternoon's projects in favour of another glass or two of that rather pleasant El Plonko.

'I'm at my wits' end about Poppet,' said my friend suddenly. 'You know her mum's gone into a home, don't you?'

Well, I couldn't deny it; I did know that the old lady had gone into a home at the splendid age of 101. What wasn't quite so splendid was the fact that the home had a "No Pets" policy, so after years of quiet and rewarding companionship, the poor woman had had to part with her elderly cat.

'I thought she had a friend who had promised to take Poppet if anything happened?' I asked, trying not to sound panicky.

'There was somebody, but she's moved away now and nobody has her contact details. Poor Poppet is alone in the flat with various people going in to feed her.'

A few days later I accompanied my friend to the flat, which seemed even emptier with the cat in it than it might have seemed if it had actually been totally empty. We gathered Poppet up, salvaged a few grubby possessions, and closed the door. We both felt sad, but kept up a merry prattle for Poppet's benefit.

It would be easy to assume that our cats are generally a bit dim, but their reaction to Poppet proved otherwise. They are actually so intelligent that they realised immediately that Poppet, Elizabeth and Whizzy, all being white with black splodges, were in fact the same cat. Sometimes Whizzy could be a different cat, but only when they could see that she had three legs. This was a huge plus as Miss Poppet slipped under the radar with hardly a spit or a grumble from the existing residents, which probably compares very favourably with the huffing and puffing that generally accompanies the arrival of a new person in a home for elderly humans.

It soon became obvious that poor old Poppet had a few health problems and a blood test confirmed that her thyroid wasn't so much overactive as manic. She fell on her food like a starving wolf and found it hard to settle, but as the trusty medication kicked in, a calmer and more confident cat emerged.

Veterinary records showed Poppet's age as a kittenish 16 years, but the microchip records revealed she was actually 22, which accorded more convincingly with her appearance. She soon commandeered a scratching tower which had been temporarily parked in the dining room and decided that the middle platform was the best position for taking full advantage of the heat from the warm air vent; it also enabled her to poke any cats foolish enough to pass directly underneath. Some people might have found it inconvenient to squeeze past the scratching tower, but one glance at that rather sulky little black and white face convinced us that we wouldn't have wanted it any other way.

More worryingly, Miss Poppet soon decided that she needed to help in the kitchen. She could see – as many have observed – that I am hardly a domestic goddess and resolved to supervise my efforts from the work top. From the work top it was but a short totter to the cooker top, where Poppet's skinny old paws ran the risk of serious injury. I did all the obvious things, like covering hot rings with pans of cold water and even tried shutting Poppet out of the kitchen, but the reproachful look when I opened the door made me feel so guilty that I realised I had to find another solution.

In the end, the answer was a lemon. Wedges of lemon, ranged along both sides of the cooker hob, produced the desired result. Poppet found the citrus smell absolutely disgusting, so would keep a respectful distance from the hot rings while maintaining a close eye on my culinary blunderings. I tried putting lemon on the borders in an effort to deter the postman from trampling my petunias into oblivion, but it didn't seem to work so effectively with him...

Clarence

The man on the phone sounded distraught and I struggled at first to understand what was happening, although it was painfully obvious that he was in the throes of a crisis.

Eventually I gathered that he had to move out of his flat and go into a group home because of severe mental problems. He had a cat that was the centre of his world, but he knew that the group home wouldn't be a safe environment for his much-loved boy. It was situated on a main road and also his fellow residents might not realise how important it was to keep the cat indoors, meaning that there was every possibility that doors and windows would be left open.

I went to collect Clarence – a huge black and white cat – and as I carried him away I heard the door slam. It didn't take too much imagination to picture his owner breaking his heart behind that door.

I felt so sorry for poor Clarence that instead of putting him into a cat pen, I installed him in our bedroom. How I ever imagined I would part with him after sharing a bed with him night after night, I have no idea. Soon it became obvious to everybody else that Clarence was here to stay and, of course, that's exactly what happened.

He was a sweet, undemanding cat of uncertain age and although he was polite to the other cats, he preferred his own company, so was happy for the most part to keep to his own quarters which just happened to be our bedroom.

However, even sweet, undemanding cats enjoy the odd moment of glory and dear old Clarence was no exception. I was getting ready to go to London for the day and seeing me in clothes other than the usual jeans and shapeless jumper must have attracted Clarence's attention. He regarded me curiously from the depths of my pillow, then hauled himself to his feet and promptly jumped onto the chest of drawers. Somehow – and I would never have thought that a cat of Clarence's considerable bulk could have achieved such a feat – he plummeted down the back of the chest of drawers and was unable to move in any direction.

Inevitably the taxi arrived to take me to the station at precisely this moment and I had to explain to a puzzled driver that I couldn't go because my cat was stuck in the bedroom.

'Why you glue cat in bedroom?' he asked, reasonably enough, in halting English.

I embarked on an explanation, but abandoned it at an early stage, pressed a fiver into his hand and breathed a sigh of relief as he drove away.

Returning to the bedroom, Clarence's penetrating cries did nothing to soothe my nerves. I tried taking the drawers out of the chest, thinking that I might be able to get him out that way, but a solid wall of wood soon ruled out that theory. Added to this, the drawers hadn't been removed – probably for centuries – so some were jammed. As Clarence's mews became increasingly desperate, I flung myself at the wretched wooden hulk and lugged it out a few inches, ruining the laminate floor in the process.

After what seemed like hours, I had made enough space for Clarence to squeeze out and could have cried with relief. My joy was shortlived, however, because the dear cat could hardly walk. The next step was to rush him to the vet's.

The vet was professional and calm. Confronted by a gibbering woman and a sorry looking cat, she diagnosed a dislocated shoulder and, with one skilful manipulation, put dear Clarence back together again.

We didn't have Clarence for very long because he was an old chap and his kidneys were already struggling when we took him in. He was a true gentleman, as was his previous owner who, in the midst of his own problems, loved his old friend enough to part with him because he wanted him to be safe.

CHAPTER TWO

Problem Cat – Or Cuddly Challenge?

Sadly many cats have pretty dreadful lives with dreadful people who should never have a pet of any sort – ever. They probably should never have children either, but this is not an opinion one can voice in polite society without attracting a great deal of criticism, if not actual physical violence.

During my cat rescuing and re-homing days, I often had reason to admire the RSPCA inspectors, who deal day in and day out with desperate situations. Although I inevitably came across distressing things, these were few and far between when measured against the satisfaction of homing a cat or kitten in a caring home, or seeing a child's face light up when a tiny kitten purred itself to sleep in his or her arms. If I came across a bad situation one day, I could always be reasonably confident that the next one would be better, unlike the RSPCA inspectors who deal with ignorance and misery on a daily basis. I hear a lot of criticism about the RSPCA, but in all fairness the law itself is a cumbersome instrument and inspectors have to do their best – often with their hands tied behind their backs in legal terms – in a far from perfect world.

However, I wouldn't want to paint too rosy a picture about the work of a Cats Protection homing officer! For example, I always wondered why it so often seemed such a good idea to a single mother with two tiny children, living in a sparsely furnished sixth floor flat, to acquire two kittens. The answer, of course, was obvious: Dillon and Kimberley wanted one each. And why shouldn't they, bless them? The answers, alas, came thick and fast. Their mother couldn't look after herself, never mind two children and two kittens; the kittens would never be able to go outside safely and there was no money available for cat food, vets' bills, cat litter, etc. But what an old killjoy I was! It would be lovely for the children and the kittens – who would obviously never grow any bigger, or ever need to empty their bladders and bowels – would be as happy as the day was long.

The fact that I would sooner have had each fingernail extracted than let these deluded people get their hands on the kittens in my cat pens did not, of course, prevent them from acquiring some wretched animal elsewhere. A modern day curse has been the availability of animals on the internet; there are also still plenty of pet shops that have absolutely no conscience about buying undernourished kittens from hopeless people who let their neglected female cats produce litter after litter just to make a few pounds. To imagine that these shops provide a caring environment for these hapless creatures, or care two-in-the-moon about the sort of home they are going to, would be naive to put it kindly.

Inevitably, a large number of kittens that have had a rubbishy start in life will end up with the animal charities – and they are the lucky ones. These little scraps would typically be handed in when they had succumbed to persistent, life-threatening diarrhoea or when they had been mean enough to vomit up a worm which, "was disgusting and I couldn't possibly have that kind of thing with the children, see?"

The unwanted adult cats generally surfaced as hungry strays, or were handed in because another animal had arrived on the scene. Sometimes, it would be due to the arrival of a baby and it often seemed as if the parents had been taken by surprise by the event, whereas most of us would have some vague idea that at the end of nine months, during which cravings for coal and/or gherkins might develop, a baby would be likely to appear. These people would never think of preparing the ground by familiarising the cat with baby noises and devising a strategy for keeping both baby and cat safe and happy *before* the big day, thus ensuring that pandemonium would inevitably ensue when baby arrived and dear old Fluffy, who was once the centre of their world, would be shoved out in the cold.

Many of the strays that came into my care were beautiful cats with sweet natures, leaving me to agonise about caring owners worrying themselves sick about their missing pet. The popularity of microchipping has dramatically increased the likelihood of lost pets being reunited with their owners, but even now many cats carry no identity and have sometimes travelled considerable distances from home, so that locally distributed posters and leaflets inevitably fail to produce the desired outcome.

Whenever a stray arrived, I would try to guess its name – a fairly fruitless enterprise, but I've always been a slow learner. I never achieved a convincing match, but as long as the cat didn't dislocate its jaw yawning as I tried "Snowy" or "Misty" in a range of voices, the poor creature would generally stuck with my first guess. New owners often changed the name anyway, so anguishing for days over an appropriate name was a bit of a pointless exercise.

A number of cats that came into my care for re-homing had problems of one sort or another; many, although they had come from the most appalling homes and were often suffering from the consequences of severe neglect, were enduringly sweet. In the following pages I tell the stories of some of the saints and sinners that it has been my privilege to know.

Beanie

The woman on the phone demanded that I took the cat immediately, if not sooner. It wasn't her cat, but belonged to her daughter's landlord some distance away. In the absence of a partner or child to vent his anger or drunkenness on, the landlord was in the habit of smacking the cat about and the caller's daughter couldn't stand it any longer. Not only that, but the landlord was away for a few days and she had the cat banged up in her bedsit.

Unfortunately, the cat pens in my garden were full and there really was nowhere that I could put the cat. I suggested other animal charities that she could contact, but she said she'd already tried everything. She would give me £50 if I would take the cat. I remember feeling extremely indignant; it wasn't about money, it was about not having the space to accommodate the poor animal.

The woman said, very quietly, 'Well we'll have to have her put to sleep then. She can't stay there and she's suffered enough.'

And so I took in little Beanie – a black and white girl with hardly any fur. Where there should have been fur, there were weeping sores and crusty scabs. Beanie had had a tough time and it showed.

I still didn't have an empty pen, of course, and at this point law-abiding cat rescuers should skip a few paragraphs, because I committed the sin of putting little

Beanie in pen with two mature and steady piebald chaps, Sammy and Bramble. It could all have gone horribly wrong, but it turned out to be a ménage-a-trois made in Heaven. The boys looked after Beanie from the start, washing her and cuddling up with her and gradually she spent less time huddling under her blanket and more time sitting on the shelf, surveying this new world where meals arrived frequently and nobody hit or kicked her.

Although her skin and coat improved, Beanie was still rather challenged in the looks department and she remained extremely frightened of strangers, so when people came to view the residents of the pens, poor Beanie did nothing to sell herself. Sammy and Bramble were elderly, which reduced their chances of finding a home, but it was Beanie who worried me most.

One morning I made the decision to adopt Beanie and took her indoors. She immediately shot behind the sofa. When I went out to the pen, Sammy and Bramble were beside themselves. They paced up and down and yowled accusingly at me, so that I found myself explaining that it was all for Beanie's own good and she would be absolutely fine. An hour later they were still pacing and yowling and I'd run out of explanations. An hour after that, Sammy and Bramble were indoors on the sofa and Beanie was thinking about emerging from her hiding place. The boys looked at each other and at me as if to say, "We wondered how long it would take you to get your act together! I suppose you can't help being a bit dim."

The three new additions settled in quickly and without upsetting the existing residents. The boys were relentlessly cheerful and Beanie seemed happy enough – in a slightly listless way. Unbeknown to me, Beanie was waiting to fall in love. And so was I – although unlike Beanie I hadn't realised.

I had been on my own for some ten years when I met a man from Bristol who came to my house for the first time one dismal February evening, arriving just as the home team had gathered for supper in my small and cluttered kitchen. At that time, the home team consisted of 15 cats, making it quite tricky to negotiate a way through to the rooms beyond. Roger, for indeed it was Roger, smiled and picked his way through the tabbies, torties and piebalds with a nonchalant smile. I have since reflected that it may have been thinly veiled panic rather than nonchalance, but it was enough to convince me that I shouldn't rule out the possibility of a future together. Apart from anything else, the cats would probably benefit from a masculine presence in their lives and I was beginning to notice that cat litter gets heavier as the years go by...

It soon became obvious that Roger was the answer to all Beanie's prayers. His soft West Country accent was music to her ears and she would snuggle up with him the moment he sat down. As Roger lived in Bristol and I was in Woking, phone calls played a big part in our burgeoning relationship and it wasn't long before Beanie realised it was her hero on the other end of the phone. After speaking to me for a few minutes, my beloved would ask me to "put Beanie on", and I would hold the phone while they "chatted". Beanie would squeak with delight and roll over, while I went through various contortions to hold the phone to her ear. After about ten minutes, I would take the phone back, only to be told that his supper was cooked and he'd ring me back later if he had time.

After two years – most of which seemed to be spent on the M4 – Roger and I got married and he moved to Woking. We were happy, but little Beanie was ecstatic. She lived for less than a year after this, but it was a happy time and we both hoped that it made up for some of the awfulness she had suffered in her past life. Many years have passed since Beanie travelled to the Great Dirt Tray in the Sky, but we still miss her more than I would ever have thought possible.

Bonnie-The-Biter

To many readers the name Walton-on-Thames no doubt conjures up images of lazy afternoons by the river and misty sunlight illuminating luxurious properties in a succession of tree-lined private roads. Much of Walton fulfils this expectation, but there are also some pockets of misery that would make the grimmer parts of the Elephant and Castle seem cheery by comparison.

One late afternoon I was driving around looking for a block of flats, only to find that "Eversley" was in fact "Heathersley". Silly Me! Having pulled myself together and found the appropriate front door, I rang the bell and fixed a smile firmly into position. The female mountain that confronted me was a frightening prospect, and one which wasn't enhanced by the soiled vest which struggled valiantly to contain two enormous, tattooed breasts.

'You 'ere to collect the frigging cat?' she asked in a threatening manner – but she probably could have made "I love you" sound pretty menacing.

'Yes. Bonnie, isn't that her name?'

In the absence of further witty repartee, I trailed in after her in time to see her scruff a dejected looking black and white cat.

'Get the bloody box open then!' she shrieked. 'Sodding thing's vicious – you won't get more than one chance to get the bugger!'

With the cat cowering in the carrier, I turned my attention to the paperwork.

'I'll need you to sign the cat into the Charity's care,' I ventured as her looming hulk blotted out the afternoon sun.

'Ain't you got enough to do then?' she responded helpfully. 'Talk about make a meal of it!'

She scrawled across the form and I headed down the concrete steps, cat carrier bumping against my legs.

Her feminine tones echoed down the stairwell. 'And you frigging well look after 'er!'

I shall not dwell on the grubby urchin draped across the bonnet of my car – a beguiling child who kicked the carrier and told me he was glad to see the back of the cat and he'd be getting a new kitten soon. I knew it wasn't his fault, of course, but with his grimy face leering at me as I drove away, I had to make a supreme effort to differentiate between the brake and the accelerator pedals.

The first few weeks in the cat pen were difficult for Bonnie and almost impossible for me. She clawed me at every opportunity and would have bitten given half an opportunity. Of course, it was only because the poor cat had come from a hellish home, but knowing this didn't make her any easier to deal with. In time she became more tolerant of me, but when any potential owner appeared, Bonnie's attitude left much to be desired.

The poor cat was in the pen for several months until I arrived home one golden afternoon in early autumn and could bear it no longer. I opened the door of the pen and after some minutes Bonnie emerged. She walked hesitantly across the grass as if she thought it might give way and it occurred to me that she might never have experienced this before, coming as she did from a concrete jungle. She rolled over, her thin little legs waving in the air, then jumped up and rushed madly round in circles.

She came indoors later that day and huffed and puffed at the other cats, then settled down and we all breathed again. Over the next few months, Bonnie progressed to the point where I could pick her up without too much difficulty, as long as I had a firm grip and didn't hesitate. Any dithering would be punished with a sharp nip or a stinging scratch. In time, she became very much my special cat and then decided that Roger was okay too.

Unfortunately, she never became reliable with visitors, achieving many impressive victories with people who thought they knew all about cats and who disregarded my well-intentioned advice to give her a wide berth. One of the more notable episodes concerned a man who insisted on jangling his car keys in front of that sharp little black and white face.

As the words, "don't worry, I know my cats", died on his lips, Bonnie crunched down on his finger and the kitchen was transformed into a war zone. Another triumph was the attack on the long-suffering RSPCA Inspector, who had dropped round to deliver two needy cats that the RSPCA was unable to accommodate. The poor woman absent-mindedly trailed her hand down Bonnie's back before I'd engaged my brain – it wasn't a pretty sight.

Another of Bonnie's little quirks was her obsession with leather. Harmless enough, you might imagine, unless you were wearing leather shoes, or were rash enough to turn up at Tresta Towers with a leather handbag, in which case you could rely on Bonnie emptying the contents over the floor. You could also rely on having to time your departure to coincide with one of Bonnie's comfort breaks – or risk incurring her wrath and some painful injuries in the process.

When Bonnie had to be put to sleep because of an aggressive tumour on her heart we were absolutely devastated. We only hope that the years she spent with us were happy. We could not have loved her more.

Lord Wispy

It is never a good idea to have a pet that is cleverer than you. I have had many cats over the years and many possessed a variety of talents, but few displayed the intellectual powers that resided in Lord Wispy's fluffy little head.

Wispy and another cat came to me for re-homing when their owner could no longer keep them and it immediately became clear that the two cats loathed the sight of each other. They were not in the first flush of youth, but appeared to be sweet tempered and before too long I had a chance to home Wispy's companion, who left for pastures new with a cheery wave of the paw and never looked back. Poor Wispy remained – a hunched, bedraggled figure of uncertain age.

I already had what would be considered by normal people to be a ridiculous number of cats, so I somehow reasoned that bringing this sad little creature in from the cold would be a sensible thing to do. I gathered him up and carried him over the threshold, whereupon he turned from sad little waif to monster in seconds. In due course he took over the kitchen work top and helped himself to anything he fancied. He never actually laid a paw on the other cats, but his staring eyes were a powerful weapon and his feline companions immediately either slumped into a coma or decided they simply had to wash their bottoms.

Wispy was white and tabby and very small, with fluffy, flyaway fur and a pretty, rather girlish face. He was able to open every cupboard door within days of arrival and soon got to grips with the fridge, listening like a safebreaker for the noise which meant that one more jerk of his skinny little white paw would give him access to untold riches. As long as he got his own way, Wispy was the sweetest cat in the world. Denied the chicken he thought he should have, he became a demon, piddling up the walls and flinging things on the floor.

He was treacherous with small children, who were inevitably fascinated by his beguiling appearance. He once made a bee-line for a small boy who was sitting perfectly quietly while his mother and I chatted and raked his claws across the child's face. I snatched Wispy up and banished him to the kitchen, where he waged a one-cat war on a bunch of bananas and a used teabag.

A blood test revealed that Wispy was suffering from an over-active thyroid and I decided to go ahead with the operation rather than have an on-going battle with tablets. Wispy breezed through the operation, returning with a neat "zip" down his chest. After a few weeks, however, although he appeared to have made a good recovery, his behaviour still left much to be desired. I returned to seek the vet's advice.

The vet listened carefully to the long list of Wispy's misdemeanours, then rocked back on his heels and said the words that made my blood run cold.

'I'm very much afraid that we must consider one other possibility,' the great man said.

'Oh no!' I gasped, 'what do you think is wrong with him? Is it something dreadful?'

The vet smiled pityingly. 'No – I think we just have to face the fact that he's a very nasty old cat!'

Greatly relieved, I hugged my ageing feline yob and took him home where his reign of terror continued without respite.

When Roger started to visit for weekends, Wispy took a charitable view, welcoming him on Friday evenings and waving him off on Sunday afternoons with hardly a twitch of the whiskers. Things took a drastic turn for the worse, however, once Roger moved in for good. If Beanie's dreams came true with Roger's arrival, Wispy seemed to feel that his fuzzy little world was about to end.

The first warning – apart from a few glares and snorts – was the early morning horror of soaking wet slippers. Wispy had piddled copiously in Roger's slippers overnight, but this was just the start of a vitriolic campaign that continued for months. Anything belonging to Roger was fair game – coats, briefcases, shoes. Another favourite was the staring game; Wispy would position himself in front of Roger and stare at him without blinking for minutes at a time, until the poor man was shuffling his feet and showing obvious signs of discomfort.

A lesser person would have buckled, or – more likely – taken the cat on a one-way trip to the vet's, but Roger was made of sterner stuff and fought back, eventually winning Wispy over with offerings of chicken and ham.

Wispy soon began to realise the rewards to be gained by playing one off against the other. He would paw at Roger's arm and gaze into his face, while flinging the odd hostile glare in my direction. Roger, anxious to capitalise on his new-found popularity, would ply the old schemer with goodies and agree with him that "Mummy had neglected him very badly, but Daddy was here now and would look after Wispy."

It was slightly inconvenient that Wispy decided to live on the cooker top, but we became adept in sliding him to one side at meal times and covering up hot rings with saucepans of water. Inevitably we had the occasional mishap, which unsurprisingly was never, ever, Wispy's fault. One particularly messy episode involved Wispy's plumed tail draping itself in the roasting tray where the fat from a serious cooking session was congealing quietly. I returned to the kitchen to find poor old Wispy struggling to get up, weighed down as he was with a tail that resembled a fat-encrusted table-tennis bat.

His elevation to the peerage in due course was inevitable given his aristocratic inclinations. People suddenly started referring to him as "Lord Wispy" and the only strange thing about it was that it hadn't happened before. I would like to say that he mellowed with age, but it would be a fib. To his dying day our much-loved tyrant did just what he liked, but we wouldn't have changed one tuft of fur on his shaggy little head.

Bella, also known as St Petersburg Cloud Princess

Another much-loved fluffy cat was a dear little pedigree Persian – a white and tortoiseshell beauty, or she would have been if she hadn't been owned by an owner from hell.

The phone rang one Sunday morning and a pleasant young woman told me she had a pedigree Persian, ten years old, that needed to be re-homed urgently. I started wittering away about it being best to contact the Persian rescue people who were likely to have a list of potential owners, whereupon the caller's voice assumed an increasingly desperate tone. She had, apparently, been trying to contact other rescue organisations without success; she had either failed to get a reply, or had been told that the cat could not be accommodated immediately and that the best they could do would be to put it on a waiting list.

I asked her why the situation was so urgent and she eventually blurted out the full, sad story. The Persian did not in fact belong to her, but she had that very day secured the owner's agreement to re-home the cat. This woman had kept the Persian in her kitchen for no less than eight years. During this time the cat had been unable to see out of any windows and had had minimal company. In response to the obvious question about why the woman had insisted on keeping the cat, the caller said that the Persian had originally belonged to her daughter, who had gone abroad to live eight years ago. For some reason, the woman had felt bound by her promise to keep the cat, even though the daughter had hardly beaten a path to her mother's door during the intervening years.

The caller had obtained the woman's signature on a statement saying that she relinquished all title to the cat and whisked the little Persian away, confident that she would be able to place her with a rescue organisation within the hour. She was unable to keep the cat herself because she lived with her parents who had a houseful of dogs, cats and, quite possibly, dinosaurs for all I know.

And so it was that this little mop arrived at Tresta Towers – tiny, terrified and tangled.

'What's her name?' I asked in as bright a tone as I could manage.

'I don't know,' said the girl. 'The woman couldn't remember what her daughter had called the cat. She's beautiful though, isn't she? Shall we call her "Bella"?'

Well, she wasn't, but we did. She hid away in the pen and I worried desperately about her. She didn't emerge to use the dirt tray, so I had no option but to change her soiled bedding several times a day to keep the fuzzy little creature as dry and comfortable as I could. She hardly ate a thing and as the weather grew colder with the onset of November, I decided to bring her indoors.

I created a tiny kingdom in a kitten pen, complete with cosy igloo bed and in a triumph of hope over experience, shoved in a fetchingly girlie pink dirt tray. At first, all we saw were clumps of white and tortoiseshell candyfloss sticking out of the igloo, but in due course we were treated to a prolonged sighting of a flat face with the most enormous eyes. This owl-like apparition fascinated the other cats and we had to make sure that little Bella was appropriately screened as over-exposure to the feline paparazzi was enough to make anybody nervous.

Meanwhile, poor Bella had to be repeatedly dragged from her igloo and carted, shivering, to the vet's because of her quite dreadful skin problems. She would huddle under a blanket in the cat carrier, only emerging to grind her poor itchy face on the bars. I would inevitably arrive at the vet's with a creature that bore a much closer resemblance to a hairy beetroot than a pedigree Persian cat. Reluctantly, the vet prescribed a hefty course of steroids to subdue the problem and soon our little fluffball was looking very much better.

By now she was a full member of the gang and was even venturing into the garden on a sunny day, where she entranced us by chasing butterflies. Needless to say, her success rate was somewhere minus zilch, but she had a lovely time "hunting".

She quite suddenly decided that as a pedigree, she should enjoy a more elevated position in the household and moved up to the dining room table. We knew better than to argue with royalty and the lopsided igloo with its fuzzy little occupant became well-loved table decorations for several years.

A blow fell when Bella was diagnosed with steroid-induced diabetes and had to have insulin injections. We worried about her skin problems returning once she stopped the steroid treatment, but coincidentally we started feeding her on a breed-specific dry food around this time with magical results. We waited with baited breath for her to start ripping at herself again, but nothing happened. In due course, a blood test confirmed that Bella was no longer diabetic. It will come as no surprise to readers to learn that every other cat – particularly the short-haired, pointy-nosed ones – also loved the new food, which just happened to be considerably more expensive than their usual diet.

By now, as is the way with cat people, we had invented a whole back history for Bella. We had decided that she was really St Petersburg Cloud Princess and had escaped from Russia with her close friend Anastasia, who had been lucky enough to get a job in Tesco's.

St Petersburg Cloud Princess remained a stranger to the dirt tray, but we knew our place and became adept at anticipating the likely location of the next shimmering puddle or bullet-like nuggets. When she eventually came to the end of her fuzzy little life, the dining table looked horribly pristine without her messy old igloo and we even missed stepping in one of her "indiscretions"! Needless to say, we're still buying Persian food...

On the face of things, the tortoiseshell cat called "JC" was not in a desperate state, but a phrase that her owner used when asking me to re-home her pet made my blood run cold.

'The thing is, I've never liked the cat. When I had her as a kitten, she was a pretty little thing, but then they all are aren't they? Then when she grew up I looked at her and thought she was quite odd-looking really with half her face being ginger and the other side black.'

'And how old is the cat now?' I asked.

'Now let me see... Kevin – he's my youngest – he's 18 this year, so JC must be 17 if she's a day. I suppose you're going to say she's too old to find a new home. I'll have her put down if you can't take her. I wouldn't do anything horrible like dump her anywhere.'

The thought of this poor cat living with this woman for 17 years and never being liked seemed sad beyond description. Not being liked is almost worse than being hated, implying as it does a cold and uncaring indifference. Did JC ever get cuddled? Did anyone ever talk to her in the special silly voice that cat-lovers use to communicate with their pets? I think the answer would have been a resounding "no".

JC had the resigned, slightly grumpy look that brindle tortoiseshells do so well. We had settled our minds to keeping her as she was a mature lady and it would have been quite tricky to find her a home; we were also conceited enough to think that we could offer her the affection that had been conspicuously absent from her previous life. The significance of her being called "JC" eluded us, as it had eluded her previous owner, who thought that "one of the kids might have called her after something on the telly". A few days after JC's arrival, we went to the theatre to see Joan Collins in an eminently forgettable production, but the evening was far from being a waste of time because we now knew beyond a shadow of a doubt that our new cat would be called "Joan Collins".

As soon as we told her this, our sad little tortie perked up and I don't think it was entirely my imagination that she seemed to move more elegantly and with a new confidence. Joan discovered the delights of the airing cupboard at an early stage and then, by some happy chance, she happened to be in the bedroom when I opened the wardrobe door. From that moment on, Joan's great ambition in life was to get into the wardrobe and have a good old rummage amongst the boxes and old clothes that had accumulated in the depths in preparation for their one-way trip to an unsuspecting charity shop.

I fear the crumpled fleeces and furred up jeans were as great a source of disappointment to our Joan as they would have been to her eternally youthful and glamorous human namesake, but at least they made a cosy bed.

As the years went by, Joan became something of a celebrity, becoming ever more sociable and confident. With the other cats, she adopted of policy of ignoring them as far as possible, but she was quite capable of administering a sharp slap if impertinent behaviour demanded it. She ventured into the garden on warm days and snoozed the afternoon away in the borders, her brindle coat glowing amongst the flattened petunias.

Many hours of entirely ridiculous amusement were generated by casual references to Joan Collins making herself comfortable on various laps, or objecting to being pinned down by an amorous Count Lucio. Like her namesake, our Joan carried her age well, with minimal fading of her striking coat and remained sprightly into her twenty-second year.

The end, when it came, was a sudden one and hit us hard. We were so sad at losing our lovely girl that we almost envied her previous owner her indifference. However, this was a very fleeting emotion; as we all know, loving anything or anybody brings with it the probability of pain and loss, but, as we also know, life in a world without love would be no life at all.

CHAPTER THREE

Wobbly Survivors

As with humans, some animals will fight to survive and others, with apparently less life-threatening conditions, will sink back into lethargy and death.

In the wild, of course, animals that are old, disabled or weak will not survive, but in our so-called civilised society we have the opportunity to give years of extra life to both animals and humans and if the quality of those extra years can be maintained I see nothing against it. But quality is important, isn't it? Some painful interventions can be justified if they are of short duration and if the patient stands a good chance of achieving a reasonable quality of life in due course, but I do not believe that a life of prolonged pain or severe discomfort can be justified for any sentient being.

It is a fortunate animal-lover who never has to make the dreadful decision to end a life when there is no longer any hope of a sustainable improvement and in my experience there are only two things that can be of any help at such a time. One is the knowledge that to end the suffering is a final act of love for a very dear friend; the second is the support given by animal-loving friends, who might not know what to say, but make it clear that they understand the depth of loss you are coping with.

The last person – and the fact they mean well somehow makes it worse – you want to encounter is the idiot who encourages you to remember that it was "only" a cat, or a dog, or a slug come to that. Grief is an intensely personal emotion and having some fool putting their own value on how you are feeling is a thousand times worse than them saying nothing at all.

Having got that off my chest, I would like to introduce you to some of the feline survivors that it has been my great privilege to meet. In each case, I believe that they have survived to lead good quality lives. Their varying traumas have limited their activities, but in a safe and caring environment they have thrived.

Personally, I have found these cats' stories both salutary and inspirational, but my main purpose in telling them is to encourage people to open their hearts to the less-than-perfect pet. There are many cat-lovers who live in situations where it would be unsafe for them to take on a free-roaming cat and a lot of people are convinced that it's unfair to confine such a free-spirited animal. For some of these people, a cat that simply could not roam freely would be the perfect solution.

If a cat is to be denied access to the great outdoors, for entirely valid reasons, it is important for it to have enough companionship and stimulation to provide a good quality of life. Often other animals will provide comfort to a wobbly or fragile companion and in my experience have shown an instinctive understanding of their less robust companion's needs. Children also seem to bond with a needy animal and learn that things don't have to be perfect to be lovable.

I should mention a group of cats that can make

wonderful indoor pets provided they can settle to a confined way of life. Cats that have been infected with the Feline Immunodeficiency Virus (FIV) can live full lives as indoor pets and with appropriate veterinary support are now often living as long as cats without the virus. Although there are close similarities between FIV and HIV, each is a species-specific virus and cannot be passed between cats and people.

Unfortunately, many FIV cats will inevitably be unneutered strays, as the virus is generally passed on by biting, and in some cases the cat has lived too long as a vagabond to settle happily to an indoor life. If this turns out to be the case, euthanasia may well be the only option. We have never given a home to an FIV positive cat simply because we have always had other cats in the household, but I have been delighted to find loving homes for some notable FIV cats in the past, one of which is featured later in this book.

It's a strange world that invests a lot of time, money and effort in breeding animals to be different and in some cases to pass on mutations which in the wild would be eradicated at an early stage, but finds it difficult to accept a cat or dog with a missing limb or a neurological impairment. I hope you agree.

Elizabeth Advising the Author

Isabelle

Elizabeth and Isabelle

The death of any animal is a sad business, but I have always struggled particularly with the loss of a tiny kitten. It is a life unlived and hope has been extinguished almost before it had flickered into being; it often seems that the tiniest pawprints leave the deepest scars on a grieving heart.

I knew that brave little Gizmo had reached the end of his very short life. The tiny black kitten had suffered a succession of fits and these had increased to the point where it would have been cowardly and cruel to allow him to continue. I wish I could say that years of rescuing cats and kittens had given me a philosophical approach to such matters, but on this sunny August evening I was in bits. The vet had done the deed and I was trying to hold a cup of tea without slopping it all over her.

'That's it,' I said. 'I've had enough of this awfulness. I tried so hard and look what's happened to that poor little soul! A couple of days ago, I really thought he was improving and then he deteriorated so quickly!'

The vet, who must have heard this sort of rambling a thousand times before, smiled and patted me on the arm.

'It's because you care,' she said. 'People like us do what we do because we care. Losing the occasional battle hurts, but it's part and parcel of what we do.'

I became vaguely aware that the poor woman would probably have liked to get home before midnight and gulped back the tea.

Instead of seizing the opportunity to leave, the vet hesitated.

'Now is the wrong time to talk about it,' she said, 'but we have a little kitten here that desperately needs to be given a chance. Perhaps we can talk about it next week? We mustn't leave things too long...'

What a clever woman she was! She knew that I wouldn't be able to leave without that kitten. And so I left with my little dead kitten to be buried in the garden, a feisty black and white mum puss and a tiny white and tabby girl kitten. The kitten and her mother had been found in an outhouse in the grounds of a local residential home and taken to the vet's. The kitten was only four weeks old and couldn't move her hind legs, which trailed behind her like tapes as she walked, propelled by her sturdy little front legs. The vet had said there was nothing that could be done for the kitten in terms of veterinary treatment; her only hope was intensive physiotherapy to activate the muscles in her back legs. While she was small her mother worked tirelessly to keep her clean, but as she grew bigger toileting would become a major problem.

I decided to install the little family in the spare room so that I could spend every spare moment working on the kitten's legs. I called her mother "Mary" and the kitten soon became "Elizabeth". That very evening I introduced Elizabeth to the delights of "cycling exercises", manipulating the limp little legs to the amazement of her mother, who soon decided that my role in life was to give her a much-needed break from this troublesome and needy brat.

The problem was that the absence of muscle tone caused Elizabeth's back legs to splay out every time I stood her up. Inspiration struck while I was engaged on an excruciatingly boring task at work the following day: I would make a passageway bounded by boxes of books. The passageway would be kitten-sized and the boxes would keep Elizabeth upright. I couldn't wait to get home to try this out and found that a sudden headache coincided with my need to leave immediately.

Mary stifled a bored yawn as I stood back to admire my invention and Elizabeth snuggled into her mother's warm fur, confident that this couldn't be anything to do with her. Seconds later, I'd placed her in the passage with her tiny white paws against the boxes.

Elizabeth looked at me and I looked at Elizabeth. It seemed forever before she twitched her pelvis and with heartrending concentration swung her hind legs a few inches along the passage. Over the next few days Elizabeth made spectacular progress, inching her way along the entire length of the passage – a distance of some four yards.

Coincidentally, two weeks after Elizabeth's arrival another kitten was brought into my care. This baby was supposed to be eight weeks old, but she resembled a small furry brick and she moved very slowly, falling over frequently and being unable to get up once she had done so. The owner had called her "Po", but obviously that was never going to do anything to encourage her to grow into a young lady, so "Po" became "Isabelle" and was introduced to Elizabeth in due course.

Unfortunately, Mary didn't see the fun of having another waif to cope with and had to be restrained from killing both kittens. It was a tricky decision to take, but it seemed likely that the two kittens would do more for each other than I could ever hope to and I therefore had Mary spayed and re-homed two weeks earlier than normal. Thankfully, Mary went to a lovely home and I suspect she never gave her funny little baby another thought.

Meanwhile, Isabelle progressed slowly, only occasionally showing a flash of kittenish behaviour before lapsing back into lethargy. The vet initially suspected some brain damage; all we could do was await developments. Elizabeth was moving well in her custom-built passageway, but her legs were still not strong enough to support her out in the open. There were days when neither kitten seemed to be progressing and I tried not to think about the obvious implications of them not achieving an acceptable level of mobility.

A dear friend of mine who visited the kittens frequently went away for two weeks and struggled to say the right thing before she left. She said she hoped that all would be well with the babies, but it had to be faced that they might not make it. Whatever happened, I had to remember that we had tried. How sensible! But I couldn't for a moment think of these adorable creatures not living their lives! I began to think of all the things I could do to cope with cats that couldn't walk or support their weight – things that I would tell other people were not to be contemplated.

One evening I was sitting in their room, conscious that they were curled up together in one of their many cosy beds. It had been a busy day and it may be that I'd dropped off. There was a sudden commotion in the corner of the room and I peered into the gloom to see two kittens knocking seven bells out of each other. Elizabeth broke free to wobble towards me, only to be jumped on by Isabelle. I know it's what kittens do, but this was different. This was a miracle.

Penny

The expedition didn't get off to a good start. I drove past the cottage on the busy road three times before I managed to pull over without some maniac smacking into the boot. Slightly ruffled, I tottered down the overgrown path and rang the doorbell. The dog inside didn't so much bark as make the Hound of the Baskerville's howl seem like a budgie having a coughing fit.

The rather vague young woman who came to the door did nothing to inspire confidence, but at least the German shepherd dog seemed to think she was in control and allowed me to enter. I had gone to collect an elderly black and white female cat who was – allegedly – a born troublemaker with dodgy toilet habits. The story was that a friend had asked the woman to look after the cat while he wandered round the world for a bit, but time had gone on and she hadn't heard from him for months now, so Blackie needed to move on.

A glance around the room failed to reveal the whereabouts of Blackie, but the search was hampered somewhat by my tendency to fall over the dog every time I took a step in any direction. The woman obviously thought she had more than fulfilled her responsibilities by letting me in and it was only after I'd come close to strangling my canine assistant that she suggested I might look behind the sofa.

Sure enough, there was a tiny black cat with white toes and bib, crouching in what looked horribly like a pile of dried faeces. I bent down to pick her up and she bit me.

'You didn't tell me the cat might be tricky to handle!' I muttered as I scruffed the unfortunate creature and shoved her in the carrier. 'I'd have worn gloves if you'd said!'

A half-hearted shrug was the response from the woman, but at least the dog rose to the occasion and howled in sympathy before charging at the carrier.

'He's never liked the cat,' the woman said, making no attempt to get the dog under control as I held the carrier aloft and headed for the door.

I put Blackie into the pen and she walked straight into the wire. She backed away from the wire and promptly walked into the steps going up to the cat house. Poor old Blackie was as blind as the proverbial bat.

I felt an overwhelming rush of sympathy for this poor cat. She had been left with a woman who seemed to struggle with the most basic concepts of pet care and forced to live with a dog that would have made a wolf look cuddly. As if this wasn't enough to cope with, this little soul was blind. I brought her indoors and put her in the spare room before picking up the phone and asking the woman why she didn't tell me that the cat was blind.

'You're kidding!' was the reply. 'Blind? She never is! What makes you think she can't see?'

I won't embarrass you, gentle reader, by detailing my response. Suffice it to say that the conversation was a short one.

The vet confirmed that Blackie had detached retinas, which meant that there was no chance of a recovery. The little cat seemed content in the spare room and soon found her way around. She was scrupulously clean and ate well, moving slowly and deliberately around the room and finding her way into her igloo bed. It must have been a huge relief to be left in peace after being pestered and terrified by the constant attentions of that rabid dog.

Over the course of the next few weeks, "Blackie" somehow became "Blind Penny" – and no, I have no idea why we felt the need to add "Blind" to her name, apart from the fact that we had had another "Penny" many years previously and this would avoid confusion in the unlikely event that anybody thought the original cat was still with us at around fifty years of age. Blind Penny had two speeds: very slow and stop. When we introduced her to the other cats, she sat down and went to sleep – a cunning tactic which threw them completely.

A surprising thing about Blind Penny was that our male cats found her overwhelmingly attractive and would vie with each other to sit next to her or to share meals with her. She was fifteen years old if she was a day, but to the boys she might as well have been a skittish fluffy kitten. Their manners generally speaking were beyond reproach, with the exception of dear Benjamin Wobble who became obsessed with grabbing her by the scruff with a view to doing unspeakable things – if only he could have remembered what they were. Needless to say, all our cats had been "adjusted" at the earliest possible opportunity, but Benjy didn't seem to realise this and had to be peeled off Blind Penny with monotonous regularity.

The old cat took everything in her very slow stride and seemed happy. She had several years of adoration before her time came to head for the Great Dirt Tray in the Sky, leaving us to mourn and a disconsolate Benjamin to cast around for another "friend". A lumpy cushion seemed to do the job – I just hope Penny didn't know.

I took in four exceptionally attractive 7-week old kittens on a Tuesday morning in early October. There were two black and white girls, one grey tabby boy and a ginger boy. The owners had kept the mother cat and had promised to get her spayed with some financial assistance from Cats Protection.

The kittens were like furry jumping beans; if they missed their mother they were certainly putting on a brave front as they swarmed up the wire, chased each other round the dirt trays and indulged in boxing matches where about one in ten swipes actually reached its target.

On Saturday mornings I had help with the pens from several tried and tested volunteers and on this particular Saturday the gang had gone out ahead of me while I dealt with a phone enquiry. A few minutes later, I collided with Toni in the doorway.

'Those two kittens are a handful, aren't they?' she laughed.

'Two?' I screeched, 'there are four in there!'

Toni looked startled. 'Well, I haven't been into the pen. I expect the other two are still in their house.'

I rushed round and flung open the door to the house. The two boy kittens were indeed in there. The ginger one was wandering round in a slightly dazed fashion and the little tabby was lying in his bed, shaking violently. He had obviously been fitting for some time as he was lying in urine and faeces.

I scooped up the whole litter and rushed to the vet's. On the way I had to think of names: the girls became Hilda and Maud, the boys Bill and Ben. And yes, I know – but names were the least of their problems! The vet's first suggestion was that the male kittens had somehow had access to something poisonous, but I knew that this wasn't possible because they had been in the cat pen since their arrival and all the cleaning materials used were cat-friendly; there were no plants within reach and the kittens only had safe toys to play with and tried and tested food to eat. The vet was mystified and said that he would hospitalise the kittens. I knew that the outlook was decidedly dodgy; fits are never good news, particularly fits of long duration.

This was the start of a nightmare. Over the next few days, the ginger kitten started fitting and lost his sight and the tabby showed very little sign of improvement. The two girls continued to bounce around their kennel in what I can only describe as a rather insensitive manner.

Numerous blood tests were carried out and the results were inconclusive, although toxoplasmosis seemed the most likely candidate, possibly contracted from their mother. Kittens tend to be vulnerable during their first few days away from their mother as they are no longer benefiting from the mother's antibodies. Although these kittens were weaned they would have still suckled from her while the opportunity was there and this would have protected them. Once they were away from her it was entirely possible that their fragile immune systems had been unable to deal with the threat.

One of the veterinary nurses gave a home to the two girls and after more than a week of drips, antibiotics and intensive nursing, I brought the boys home and installed them in the spare room. The tabby, Billy, showed no sign of any impairment, but ginger Ben was very wobbly on his skinny little legs, although mercifully his sight had returned. Our jubilation at their return was shortlived; two days later, both kittens had gone down with cat flu.

Billy recovered quickly, but Ben became dangerously ill for the second time in his short little life. He could hardly breathe and I spent long periods in the bathroom holding his tiny emaciated body over a steaming basin of water. He wasn't interested in food, so it was a case of syringing down an unappetising cocktail of food and drugs at all hours of the day and night. One morning I took up my usual position on the floor and filled the syringe from a saucer. As I touched his mouth with the tip of the syringe, a tiny ginger paw pushed it away.

I knew then that little Ben had had enough. The kind thing would be to let him sleep and let Nature take its course. I settled him on to my lap and must have drifted into an exhausted doze because the next thing I was aware of was a small ginger kitten wobbling towards the saucer and making a valiant effort to lap up the gloopy grey mess. Our little ginger soldier had decided to live.

We adopted both kittens – of course! – and had to keep reminding ourselves that their early problems had caused significant damage and we should see every day with them as a bonus. However, the loss of Billy from a massive fit at the age of 18 months was horribly sudden and no attempt to rationalise his death helped us one bit.

Around this time, Benjamin Wobble, as he had become, embarked on a rather reckless expedition. Anybody who has lived through the agonising experience of trying to trace a missing cat will probably nod knowingly when I say that it rarely does much for relationships and it was certainly touch and go with Poor Roger and I as to whether we killed each other or simply headed for the divorce courts.

Benjamin disappeared through a hole under the back fence on a chilly Thursday in February. The temperature was around minus seven degrees at the time and the thought of our disabled wobbly boy wandering the woods drove us mad. We searched day and night, we phoned every vet, every charity, the microchip people, the police, the refuse collectors, all to no avail. We stuffed leaflets through doors, put up posters and accosted unsuspecting people in the street. Sunday morning came and we had still heard nothing.

We knew by now that we were likely to be looking for a body rather than a live ginger cat, but by that stage we were desperate for any news and resolved to search the woods inch by inch until we had found something. We split up in order to cover more ground and after nearly two hours I had the strangest sensation of calm. I stood in a small glade and thought how wonderful it would be if I turned round and saw Benjamin.

I turned round and there, some hundred yards away, was a wobbly ginger cat.

Benjamin is nearly eight years old now. He is on medication to reduce the incidence of fits, but is a happy boy with more love to give than can easily be contained in his cuddly ginger body. We still have our moments, but any worries are more than offset by the joy of sharing our lives with such a very special boy.

Stumpy Malone

Some years ago, probably when we'd overdone the gardening, Poor Roger and I took the decision that we had reached the stage where it would be foolish to have any more kittens. This is not a euphemism for children – they were never on the agenda.

As well as the aches and pains that coincided with entitlement to winter fuel allowances and free bus passes, we were influenced by the number of cats we had adopted that had lived well into their twenties. This led us to think that any kitten we adopted at this juncture might well live to see the establishment of a Cats Protection Branch in a hitherto undiscovered galaxy; there was certainly every possibility that he or she would be skittering around long after we had fallen off our perches.

Fortunately, no sooner had we arrived at this dangerously rational decision than a heaven-sent excuse presented itself for us to do exactly the opposite. We heard that a stray mother cat had been found living with her kittens down the side of a garden shed. The mother cat and her two surviving babies were rounded up by the local Cats Protection volunteers, who also removed a tiny dead kitten. The two kittens – one tabby, one black – were lively enough, but the little black baby had a problem with his back legs. Upon closer inspection it became obvious that he had been born without hind paws.

We heard about "Stumpy" and a thought began to dawn – a thought that rapidly hardened into an obsession when we heard that his tabby brother, "Woody", had been homed, but people were worried about adopting a kitten without back paws. This gave us the excuse we were looking for; we could give Stumpy the safe environment he needed and we were around a lot to keep an eye on those vulnerable little back legs. I was due to have a hip replacement, so it would obviously be sensible to get that out of the way before taking on a kitten.

However, we've never been very sensible, so a few weeks before I had the operation young Stumpy arrived. For some reason he became "Stumpy Malone" at an early stage – just because it seemed to suit him. I returned from hospital on crutches, which fascinated Stumpy, who charged between them and my legs at every opportunity so that I became adept at keeping my balance and amazed the 12 year old physiotherapist who had the dubious privilege of running the "hip class" in subsequent weeks.

We were very worried about letting our boy outside in case the ends of his hind legs became sore, but it soon became obvious that he was desperate to venture forth. Since Benjamin's great escape and the ensuing drama, we had taken steps to make the back garden escape proof to anything other than the most agile cat, so we were confident that Master Malone would be safely confined.

He was thrilled to be outside and spent hours chasing leaves, flies and anything that moved. The ends of his little hind legs calloused over and he showed no sign of discomfort. He was slower than cats with back paws and couldn't climb properly, but in the main he was able to do everything that a self-respecting cat needs to do, including upsetting the girls by jumping on them when they were engaged in the serious business of toilet activity.

We would often see him hanging from branches, his short little back legs dangling, and would rush out in a vain attempt to catch him before the inevitable plummet. On grass or carpet Stumpy would walk on all fours, but on concrete or on wooden floors he perfected the art of walking on his front two paws, proving – if proof were needed – that it takes more than a few missing bits to keep a plucky little cat down.

We always made sure that Stumpy was indoors before darkness fell; our rear garden has always been popular with foxes and our boy would certainly not have had the turn of speed necessary to get away from a hungry and determined fox. All went well until one evening when we searched in vain. I became convinced that he was under the summerhouse, having seen him disappear under there earlier in the day, and spent a frustrating hour or two dangling an array of fishing rod toys in what I hoped was a tempting manner.

By eleven o'clock there was still no sign of our hero. My summerhouse theory was looking decidedly flaky and my dangling had lost some of its conviction. Although we knew he couldn't possibly have climbed the fence, Poor Roger decided to have a look out the front. There, nonchalantly washing his face, sat Stumpy Malone.

This would not happen again – Poor Roger would make sure of that. The next day, numerous plastic panels were attached to our side of the fences to make climbing – especially with half the usual complement of paws - virtually impossible.

Later that summer we were relaxing in the lounge and the outside light came on. It was after midnight and we were waiting for the badgers to come for their usual running buffet. We were laughing at Evie, our lively black girl, who was chasing moths and having a wonderful time. She was soon joined by another black cat of a similar size. For a moment I thought it was Stumpy, but we knew he was asleep in his igloo bed.

Except he wasn't, of course. He must have nipped out when one of us popped outside and had probably been having the time of his life for several hours.

Stumpy is four years old now and we still worry about him. He is as kittenish as ever and very, very naughty, which is just how a kitten should be. He doesn't know that he has a disability; in fact, he probably wonders why other cats have those funny blobby things on their back legs. In his furry little way he is an inspiration and an endless source of joy.

Tiny

I was poking unenthusiastically at a rock-hard baked potato when I realised my companion was asking me a question.

'Tell Maggie about all your Special Needs cats!' he said. 'She'd love to hear about them, I know.'

The three of us were enjoying a brief respite during a punishing day. We were at a large school in Essex delivering talks about Cats Protection and cat care to children who occasionally surfaced from a comatose state to yawn in our faces. Maggie – a kind person – smiled politely and probably regretted it almost immediately as I launched into a spirited account of Benjamin Wobble's latest antics.

John, who had met the Tresta Towers cats, abandoned his lunch and cleared his throat.

'The cat I feel sorry for is little Tiny,' he said.

It was a war of nerves. Maggie departed to get a drink of water and in her absence I cracked.

'Why? What's happened to Tiny?' I asked – foolishly, as it turned out.

'She's been at the vet's surgery where my wife works for nearly three years now. They've tried to home her several times, but each time she's been brought back. The thing is, she has to be shut in a cage when patients are there because she goes up to them and upsets them.'

'But she has plenty of company, surely?'

'Not really. By the time the patients have all gone, the vets and nurses are going home too, so poor Tiny is alone a lot of the time.'

'What sort of problems does she have? And how did she come to be at the vet's?' I asked.

'She was found wandering the streets and was taken in there. They couldn't trace an owner and she wasn't microchipped, so she's been there ever since. She's quite deaf and has very slight brain damage, but she's a pretty little thing.'

'Well – we weren't exactly looking to take on another cat, but I suppose we could give her a try. I still can't understand why nobody would give her a home...'

'I think it's because she's unhappy, but she has had a few toileting issues,' he admitted.

By now, of course, I was desperate to have Tiny and if he'd said she would pee all over my bed every day I wouldn't have taken any notice. John couldn't believe his luck and embraced me warmly – no doubt imagining the stunned and admiring look on his wife's face that evening when he let slip this cheering news.

A few weeks later, Poor Roger and I went to collect Tiny from the vet's practice in Sidcup. She was a stunning little tabby, but we would have loved her if she'd had a crumpled ear and one eye. She was amazingly well-behaved in the car, used as we are to non-stop yowling, projectile vomiting and fountains of pee, all of which generally occur before we've reached the end of our cul-de-sac.

We started Tiny off in a kitten pen in the lounge so that she could get used to the other cats and after a few days we let her out to mingle with her new family. At this point, Tiny transformed herself into a heat-seeking missile and made a bee-line for poor Benjamin Wobble, chewing at him and towering over his prone ginger body. We tried again a couple of days later and she targeted Stumpy Malone, sending him scuttling behind the sofa as fast as his two paws would carry him.

This was never going to work. We could put up with inappropriate toileting, but seeing our Special Needs cats traumatised by this miniature tiger was an entirely different matter. I contacted the veterinary nurse who had cared for Tiny and told her that I was desperately sorry, but we wouldn't be able to keep Tiny after all. She was absolutely sweet about it, which made me feel suicidal, and said she quite understood and we could bring Tiny back whenever it suited us. At this point I heard a voice – strangely like my own – gibbering away about possibly waiting a few more days and seeing how things went.

Everybody – including Tiny – knew that she would never be going back to Sidcup. We found a solution to the heat-seeking missile obsession by keeping her away from the others and making sure she had plenty of human company. It soon became obvious that Tiny loved people and before long she was approved as a Pets as Therapy cat and would visit care homes to be fussed and feted. She also accompanied me when I gave Cats Protection talks to schools and pensioner groups, acquiring star status.

I soon realised there was much truth in the old adage, "Never work with children or animals" because I could have been reading out a shopping list while Tiny was flinging herself after her laser light toy, or pouncing on a

Lenny Lion toy as squealing children trailed it round their classroom. Even if the talks didn't quite follow the standard format, Tiny was a peerless ambassador for the feline race and never more so than when we visited children who were frightened of animals, because it's very hard to laugh and be scared at the same time. With elderly people, she showed an instinctive awareness of their frailty and would rub against their papery skin while they smiled at the softness of her tabby fur.

Tiny has been with us for two years now. She is a very special cat with a huge amount of love to give and, in the grand scheme of things, what's a bit of inappropriate toileting between friends?

CHAPTER FOUR

The Kindness Of Cat Lovers

It would be entirely wrong of me to give the impression that I'm the only person to give a home to needy or "difficult" cats, because nothing could be further from the truth. I have simply been in the privileged position of having a large number of cats in my care which has enabled me to see who would be likely to fit in with the existing team; most of the cats that I've adopted have been elderly, disabled or have had toileting issues. The inappropriate toileting problem is obviously a significant difficulty if there are babies or young children crawling around, or if the home is regularly featured in one of the glossier magazines, but as neither applies to Tresta Towers, it really hasn't been anything that a liberal scattering of puppy pads and the odd burst of energetic cleaning couldn't deal with.

In my time as homing officer for Woking and District Branch of Cats Protection, I met thousands of people and I can honestly say that although the dreadful ones were indeed ghastly beyond belief and stuck in the memory, there were far more kind and caring people and we should celebrate this loudly and frequently. For every potential owner who wanted a cat to match their decor, there were many who would give a home to a needy little soul regardless of colour or looks; for everyone who wanted a guarantee that the cat would sit on their laps within seconds of arrival, there were lots who understood that many animals coming into Cats Protection care had suffered traumas and would need time to regain any semblance of trust in the human race.

Some people were just amazing. There was a wonderful lady who said she wanted to adopt two cats that other people were unlikely to want. I asked when she would like to come to see the cats I had and she said she didn't need to do that; she would appreciate it if I could just take them over. I arrived with two middle-aged and extremely nervous girls who had had a dreadful time with an owner who couldn't look after herself, never mind take care of her cats. Their new owner had everything ready and welcomed the girls as if they were the most beautiful creatures she had ever seen – which, of course, after several months of love and care they undeniably were.

The cats featured in the following pages are just a few of the characters who found exceptional owners, many of whom have become close personal friends. A common theme was the willingness of these owners to recognise the needs of the cat and to invest time and patience in those critical early stages. We may think that a cat understands everything we say, but in our heart of hearts we know that most cats have a rather restricted vocabulary. This inevitably means that a new owner has to show, rather than tell, the cat that they will be safe; that food will appear at regular intervals and that there will be warm places to sleep and to hide in when everything gets a bit too much.

There is no great expertise required. The things that

true cat people have in common are an ability to empathise with a nervous or stressed-out animal and a willingness to make room in their homes and in their lives to accommodate its needs. And let's not forget love; love will overcome any number of setbacks, knowing that at the end of the trials and tribulations there will be a purring pussycat and a very happy person.

Frank

Frank was trapped by Cats Protection volunteers who were searching for a missing white cat and had responded to reports of a marauding cat who was terrorising the local moggies and stealing their food.

Frank was white – give or take the odd oily patch – and very, very large. He had the most strikingly blue eyes – think Frank Sinatra – and was a handsome chap in a roguish kind of way. He gave every impression of being a feral cat, but nobody would be at their best crouched in a cold steel trap.

It was immediately obvious that Frank was an unneutered tom, so he was whisked off to the vet's for the appropriate adjustment to be carried out. He was also bloodtested for two very nasty feline diseases – feline AIDs and feline leukaemia. Unfortunately, poor old Frank tested positive for FIV – Feline Immunodeficiency Virus, or feline AIDs as most people call it. This presented us with a problem, because Frank could not simply be released as FIV can be transmitted to other cats, usually by biting, and if he was a true feral cat he could not be incarcerated for the rest of his life.

We decided to give Frank the benefit of the doubt and see how he shaped up in a cat pen. If he remained resolutely wild, there would be no alternative but to have him put to sleep.

It so happened that when Frank arrived, there was

no pen available and I therefore had no option but to bang him up in a cage in the garage. This was far from satisfactory, of course, but infinitely preferable to being dead. Every time I opened the cage to feed Frank, or to clean out the dirt tray, full of deposits that would not have disgraced an Irish Wolfhound, he flung himself to the back of the cage, crouching and snarling.

After a few days a pen became available, but Frank wasn't going to make things easy. There was no way that he was going to emerge from the cage with his paws up and I had no choice but to leave the door open and hope to catch him in the Aladdin's cave that was the double length garage. When I went back into the garage, Frank had vacated his bijou residence and gone to earth.

I was confident that baiting the trap would do the trick, but days passed and the trap remained empty. I eventually realised that Frank was helping himself to biscuits, having ripped a hole in the bottom corner of a large bag. It was clear that more positive action was required – the sort of action that owed more to desperation than strategic planning.

It was hopeless trying to round up Frank on my own, even if I'd managed to locate him, so I persuaded my friend Steve to help. We were in the garage for a very long time, getting hotter and hotter, and were just beginning to think that Frank must have tunnelled his way out when a grubby white cat shot out from the depths and raced up and down. He was obviously terrified and so were we, but Steve managed to grab him and as the blood oozed through his gauntlets, shoved poor old Frank into the cat carrier.

The gauntlets never quite recovered and Steve was a bit delicate for a while, but we had achieved the objective and soon Frank was ensconced in a luxury cat pen where he continued to snarl and spit, but at least he had plenty of room to do it. He was a magnificent cat and after a month with plenty of food and warm bedding he looked absolutely stunning. It was hard to know whether he was a true feral or whether he had just been fending for himself for a very long time, but he deserved to be given the benefit of the doubt.

It would be something of an understatement to say that there wasn't a queue forming to take Frank on. His flattened ears and bared teeth were on the scary side of cuddly and there was no way of knowing if he would ever settle as an indoor cat. After a while, poor old Frank was beginning to look depressed and I wasn't feeling very optimistic about his future either.

A young woman phoned to ask about adopting and explained at an early stage that she would have to have an indoor cat because her flat was on a busy road. At that time I had a few cats that would have fitted the bill and invited her along to see them. She was very young, very glamorous and was sweet with the cats. As we walked past Frank's pen, she asked if she could go in to see him. I explained that we didn't know what we were going to do with him because of his wild behaviour and how I had no idea whether he would ever make an indoor pet. None of this fazed my young friend, so in she went while I hovered nervously outside.

She did just the right thing. While Frank crouched at the back of his house, Tessa stood just inside the pen and blinked slowly at him.

'He is magnificent,' she said at last. 'I would love to have him if you think he'd be happy in our flat.'

I put the worst case scenario to her: he might not settle, his health might deteriorate, he might do untold damage and nobody could guarantee whether they would ever be able to stroke him. She smiled sweetly and said she was sure everything would be fine and anyway he should be given a chance.

Thrilled though I was, I hardly slept a wink the night before taking Frank to his new home. Getting him into the cat carrier wasn't easy, but it was all the "what ifs" that were running through my mind. When I arrived, everything we'd talked about had been done; Frank had a whole village of cardboard boxes to hide in, toys to play with and a running buffet to feast on when he felt peckish. Tessa was on Cloud Nine and I hoped against hope that all would be well.

There's something about, "Cometh the hour, cometh the woman," and Tessa was certainly that woman. I heard nothing for a week or so and hesitated to phone. Just as I was screwing myself up to make that call, a photograph of Frank came winging through the ether. He looked as handsome as ever and was sprawled across her husband's lap.

Griselda

There are people who have to part with their pets for very genuine reasons, such as a new baby being seriously allergic to it or when an elderly person has to move into a care home and cannot take the pet, but there are also those who tell a load of porkies that a child of three would see through.

The man who dumped Griselda and ran was not a nice person. He had told me he had to move abroad with his job; he had also told me that it was breaking his heart to part with the cat and that he would make a substantial donation to the charity. When he arrived with her, he literally deposited the carrier and ran. I was unable to trace him from details he'd provided, which was more than just a nuisance because I would dearly have liked to obtain some more information about the cat.

I took Griselda into the pen and opened the carrier. She lashed out at me with an elegant, chocolate-coloured paw, but there were no claws. This was not due to restraint on the part of my new furry friend, but to the fact that she had been declawed. This meant she had almost certainly been brought over from America as declawing is against the law in the UK – and rightly so. She made a spirited attempt to bite before scurrying into the depths of the cat house and, with one final and desperate growl, dived under a blanket.

Griselda was a striking looking cat with a plush golden-cream coat, chocolate "points" and blue eyes. She was, however, relentlessly aggressive which spoke volumes about the life she had led. I struggled to get in and out of the pen without being attacked and despaired of finding her a home. She hated the sight of other cats and whenever any of the Special Needs Unit wobbled round to the pens, she would fling herself against the wire and swear at them until they wobbled out of view. There was obviously no possibility of her being homed with any other animals or with children and it was hard to imagine anybody putting up with her behaviour, even if she had good reasons for being like it.

Once again, however, at the darkest hour a glimmer of light appeared when a pleasant-sounding couple contacted me about the possibility of adopting a cat. They had suffered a sad loss recently and weren't sure whether it was a bit too soon to take on another pet, but would like to come and see the cats in the pens to see how they felt.

They were very taken with Griselda and wanted to go in to see her. I knew that if they did, Griselda would be more than likely to scupper her chances of finding a home with them, so I explained that she was very stressed in the pen as it was a rather claustrophobic environment for a highly strung animal. The couple looked at each other and for a moment I wondered if I'd said something totally inappropriate.

'My wife suffers from claustrophobia,' said the man. 'People don't understand what a difficult thing it can be, do they, Darling?'

'I've had some terrible experiences!' said "Darling" with feeling. 'I just won't go on tube trains now – I used to try not to make a fuss, but it always ended up with me passing out or vomiting...'

Her husband interrupted, for which I was grateful. The last thing we needed was projectile vomiting – by "Darling" or by Griselda.

'So we do realise what that poor cat is going through. I think we'd like to give her a home, wouldn't we, Darling? I'm sure she'll settle down with us. It's a very quiet home – just the two of us and we'll keep her indoors, of course, because she wouldn't be able to defend herself with those poor little floppy front paws.'

The thought of the formidable Griselda being unable to defend herself required a considerable leap of the imagination, but I managed to smile encouragingly and moved swiftly towards finalising the arrangements.

The following week I marched purposefully to the pen with the firm intention of banging up Griselda in a substantial cat carrier without getting my face redesigned. An hour later, the carrier was empty and Griselda was showing no sign of tiring. It was time to abandon any thoughts of doing things by the book and give full rein to desperation; arming myself with a cardboard shield, I somehow eased the spitting, snarling bundle into the carrier.

'I think Griselda might take a little while to settle,' I chirped as I released the scowling cat into the lounge. 'I think the journey's upset her a bit.'

I suspect that this lovely couple could see through the cat rescuer's equivalent of estate agent-speak with their eyes closed, but they smiled pluckily and reassured old Grizzles that this would always be her home and there was all the time in the world to get to know each other.

The reports were encouraging. By the third week, Griselda was only biting them a couple of times a day. They were besotted with her and thought they were the lucky ones to have such a beautiful cat.

I think old Grizzles had done rather well for herself too.

Dennis

There are big cats, enormous cats, and Dennis-sized cats which are only marginally smaller than your average puma.

I was all set to deliver my standard lecture on coping with cats when a new baby comes along when I realised that the woman on the doorstep looked as if she might give birth before I'd reached the end of the first sentence. She was accompanied by a distraught man struggling to lift an exceptionally heavy cat carrier.

The lighting in the cat pens was less than brilliant and the man was anxious to say his fond farewells to his beloved Dennis, so I only had a vague impression of a rather large white and tabby cat. The couple came inside to complete the necessary paperwork and I could see how inappropriate my bracing speech would have been. Dennis had belonged to the man for several years and had always been jealous. When his new partner moved in, Dennis' jealousy had manifested itself in some fairly unpleasant behaviour. The poor woman had suffered in silence until she became pregnant. As the months went by, she had become increasingly nervous about the imminent birth and what Dennis might do to the baby.

It seemed that Dennis had formed an unnaturally close bond with "Daddy" to the point where his one aim was to eliminate any competition. The couple told me how Dennis liked nothing better than to sit on

Daddy's lap and to suck at his face, growling at the woman every time she approached. I think that secretly Daddy had rather enjoyed this adulation, but the pigeons had certainly come home to roost now.

I still secretly thought that it was very unlikely that a cat would actually kill a baby, but revised this opinion rather rapidly when I saw Dennis in daylight. He was a *very* large cat indeed.

I always thought that whoever designed the cat pens was either a person with a misplaced sense of humour or someone who had absolutely no experience of looking after cats. The shelf on which cats always sat was at face height by the door, thus maximising the possibilities of being swiped smartly round the chops on entering the pen. The first morning I went breezing in with Dennis' breakfast, he slammed me with a punch that wouldn't have disgraced Mike Tyson and I ended up wearing most of the contents of the dish.

I tried to explain to this enormous brooding presence that it would all be for the best and being nasty to me wasn't going to get him anywhere. I could tell he appreciated the wisdom of what I was saying when he crouched down on the shelf and threatened to spring at me. It was time to make my apologies and leave.

We struggled on with the relationship improving marginally, but Dennis was far too "spirited" for me to risk people going in to see him. Once again, we needed a very special owner who could see beneath Dennis' rather sullen exterior to the spoilt unhappy cat he really was.

I was having lunch with a very dear friend who always asked about the cats in the pens and I mentioned Dennis.

'I have to say he's the biggest cat I've ever clapped eyes on,' I said, 'and I've seen a few cats over the years.'

Sandy put down her knife and fork. 'Is he really big? I've always loved big cats!' she said.

I felt a rush of excitement. She came to see Dennis and wasn't at all put off by his appalling language and general rudeness. She would love to have him and fully realised that he would need a lot of patience and understanding. I told her everything, including the face suckling, but nothing fazed her – thank goodness!

I took Dennis to her and he immediately hid behind the sofa – and stayed there for a very long time.

Over the next few months it became obvious that Dennis was a compulsive bonder – and a nervous wreck. He decided that Sandy was the centre of his furry world and left nobody wondering how he felt about visitors to the house. Dennis would take up his position on the stairs and dare anybody to pass him, raking their ankles if they did. Viewed from the bottom of the stairs, Dennis appeared even larger and would certainly have sent an intruder rushing from the house.

After many years, Dennis became old and fragile and suffered from chronic pancreatitis – a horrible disease requiring sustained and demanding nursing which Sandy unquestioningly gave him. She was heartbroken when the time came to part with her big silly boy – and what a lucky boy he was to be so loved throughout his long and happy life.

Monica

I came back from the holiday feeling well-rested and ready for anything. Anything except Monica, that is.

While Poor Roger and I had been loafing around, various friends and colleagues had been involved in looking after the cats and finding homes for the Cats Protection residents and as usual I couldn't wait to go out to the pens to see what changes had occurred during our absence. There were some wonderful kittens and an assortment of adults; in the first pen there was a dark brindle tortoiseshell rejoicing in the name of "Monica" and I was puzzled to see a note on the door exhorting me, and presumably the rest of the world, to "be careful".

I went into the pen, wondering what form my being careful should take, and reached out a tentative hand to stroke Monica. The reaching out bit seemed to be acceptable, but when I withdrew my hand young Monica slashed me. She showed no signs of remorse; in fact, she looked quite keen to have another go.

I installed a Feliway diffuser in the hope that it would calm her down, but if anything it seemed to make her worse. I sought guidance from various behavioural experts, who provided various helpful hints such as wearing boots to avoid her biting and scratching my legs, and gloves to protect my hands. My favourite piece of advice was being told not to antagonise her, so I immediately stopped poking my tongue out and calling her rude names.

Monica was definitely not a feral cat. She was far too confident and the clincher was that when the vet opened her up for spaying, she was found to have been already spayed. Once again, any number of polite cats and beguiling kittens came and went, but Monica was becoming a fixture in Pen Number One.

It was a friend who gave our problem girl her chance. I was discussing the possibilities of Jenny doing some fostering for Cats Protection and mentioned that her rural location might be suitable for locating a cat that wasn't a true feral, but was proving relentlessly aggressive in the pen. I wondered if she could chat with neighbours and see if anyone would be prepared to let Monica take up residence in their garden.

'I could take her myself,' said Jenny. 'I could try her indoors and if that didn't work out, she could live in my garden.'

I pictured Monica's miserable little brindle face and was tempted.

'But you've got young girls and a dog and several cats!' I wailed, sensing defeat even as I tasted the possibility of victory. 'Monica would kill them! I'd never forgive myself!'

'She can't be that bad!' said Jenny in a patient voice. 'Being in a pen is a very unnatural environment. She'd probably blossom in a proper home.'

I succumbed to temptation.

'But you must make sure that you start Monica off in a room away from the children and away from the other pets,' I cautioned. 'And it would have to be very much a trial homing – it might not work out, we must be prepared for that.'

'Of course. You really mustn't worry so much. I've had animals all my life and I'm sure we can cope with another one.'

I could say no more, so on the appointed day I arrived with Monica, having wrestled her into the cat carrier and shoved my blood-soaked gauntlets in the washing machine.

Jenny and the girls were in a state of excitement.

'You lead the way!' I said brightly. 'Where did you think would be best for Monica to go?'

Jenny nipped ahead while I lugged the carrier up the stairs. She flung open the door of a small bedroom which was more pink than I would have ever thought possible. There were pink toys, arranged in family groups, pink walls and a pink bedspread adorned with pink roses. My blood ran cold.

'But this must be one of the girl's rooms!' I stammered.

'Yes – we talked about it and my daughter was very keen to have Monica with her. It'll be good for Monica to have company – we couldn't bear to shut her away in a room all on her own.'

I gibbered away about the dangers, only to be met with smiles and endless reassurances. Obviously Jenny thought I was overreacting to the point of madness. In the end, I opened the carrier and Monica skipped out to survey her pink palace.

I didn't sleep well that night, tormented as I was by dreams of blood-soaked bedspreads and lacerated pink teddies. Days went by and I heard nothing. In my wilder moments I pictured Monica standing on top of a pile of mangled bodies, a sardonic smile on those thin black lips.

When Jenny did ring I could hardly hear what she was saying for hyperventilating.

'Yes – she's a character, isn't she? She loves the children and isn't at all frightened of the dog, but she's certainly not keen on the other cats! Still, they'll sort themselves out. I'll send you a photo of her sitting in the dog's bed – she's really made herself at home! We all love her to bits.'

Daphne and Deirdre

I didn't know much about the two cats that were brought to me by the local RSPCA Inspector, but that was probably just as well. They were two middle-aged sisters with the most appalling skin problems. They were white and tabby in colour, but large areas of their bodies were furless and the skin was red and raw. It was hard to tell whether this was the result of an allergic reaction or self-harming due to stress, but whatever the cause these poor cats were in a terrible state.

Both cats were quite nervous, but they settled quickly in the pen and ate well. The vet prescribed steroid treatment to calm the skin irritation and we applied flea treatments as the commonest cause of skin problems is an allergic reaction to flea saliva. At least the condition didn't get any worse, but neither was there a marked improvement. Being the cheery soul I am, I quite thought that Daphne and Deirdre would take root and end up living with me, although a multi-cat household was unlikely to be the best option for such nervous girls.

It is often a joyous thing to be wrong, and never more so than when anticipating the worst.

'We're interested in adopting a pair of cats – girls if possible – and we don't mind about age or colour. There is one stipulation, however, and I hope you won't think we're being unreasonable...'

Daphne

Deirdre

Here we go, I thought. This is where they suddenly say they must have pedigree Norwegian Forest cats, or Champion Siamese cats with pink and green points.

'Tell me what you're wanting and we can talk about it,' I said, preparing to delete them from my list of hopefuls.

'Well, we would like to take two cats that are really needy and that you would struggle to find homes for. We have all the time in the world to spend with them now we're retired and we don't mind if they're nervous or a bit peculiar!'

'How would you be with problem skin?' I squeaked, convinced that this would be the deal-breaker.

'Well it won't always be a problem, will it? I expect all the poor things need is a nice home and plenty of love. No – we'll be fine with that.'

I took the two girls to their new home and they immediately disappeared behind the television. To their eternal credit, the new owners were not at all perturbed by the lurching of the television as the cats struggled for concealment – they were only concerned in case the cats hurt themselves.

I left the couple crawling across the floor to reassure themselves that the cats were safe and comfortable and hoped against hope that all would be well.

A few weeks later I was invited round to see how things were going.

'We think their skin is better, but we see them every day and it would be nice to see what you think.'

There was no sign of either cat when I went in, but I was told that they would appear once everybody sat down. Sure enough, two little heads soon appeared from behind the sofa, followed by two silky bodies. I couldn't believe my eyes. The transformation was incredible.

'They look wonderful! Are they still having the same dose of steroids?' I asked.

'No. They're not having any treatment now. I've been putting a few drops of cod liver oil in their food and grooming them with a very soft baby brush and that seems to have done the trick. Do you think they look better?'

Well, that lovely lady might well have been working miracles with her cod liver oil and her baby brush, but I think there was a more compelling reason for Daphne and Deirdre looking so wonderful. Those cats were loved – probably for the first time ever – and that's what I'd put my money on every time.

Posh Paws and Ben

The two shorthaired black cats were that rare thing – they were grateful for a warm billet with regular meals. They were also affectionate and undemanding, this last quality being something of a novelty at Tresta Towers.

The girl cat rejoiced in the rather sweet but cumbersome name of Posh Paws and her brother, a bulky, slightly dim-looking specimen, was called Ben. They were around twelve years of age and had obviously been well loved by their elderly owner. At an early stage I began to think that they might well settle happily with me, so my efforts to find them a home were less than energetic.

In due course, I adopted them and while they were indoors things jogged along quite satisfactorily. The rest of the cats didn't take much notice of the new arrivals, being well-used to comings and goings, and Posh Paws and Ben ate well and seemed happy. Sadly, it was a very different story when they ventured into the garden. Nobody took much notice while they were pottering about outside, but when they tried to come back indoors our usually placid cats made it quite clear that they thought Posh Paws and Ben should remain outside – for years, if necessary.

I carried them in and once again everybody settled down, but the next day the same thing happened. As time went on, the situation deteriorated to the point where the newcomers were hiding at the bottom of the garden and the remaining cats – scenting victory – asserted their authority more overtly. This could not be allowed to go on because it was blindingly obvious that dear old Ben, although he was the feline equivalent of the Incredible Hulk, had no intentions of sorting anybody out, or even looking them in the eye.

A lovely lady phoned and said she wasn't at all fussy, but she would like a pair of cats who were used to being together and she would like them to be young, friendly and preferably not black. Well, one out of three isn't bad and she came to see Posh Paws and Ben who were by this stage recovering their composure in one of the outdoor cat pens.

Those dear cats did everything they could – short of shedding a few years and changing colour – to persuade our guest that they should come to live with her and her husband. There are times when it's appropriate to push one's luck and times when a more sensitive approach is called for. On this occasion even I, never noted for my sensitivity, realised it would be a good idea to melt away and leave Posh Paws and Ben to work their furry magic.

When I returned, magic had definitely been worked and a week or so later Poor Roger and I took our two beautiful black babies to their new home. I well remember trying to complete the paperwork and finding it hard to see what I was doing. It was a wonderful home for Posh Paws and Ben, but we had grown ridiculously fond of them and parting was a very hard thing to do. I also felt a failure because we had usually succeeded with integrating quite tricky cats into the home team and I can only think that the togetherness of the two newcomers might have been a factor, or it could have been that they were just too sweet to stick up for themselves the first time one of the others called them a rude name.

At last the forms were completed and signed in all their scrawly dampness and I prepared to leg it out of the door. Poor Roger had felt a pressing need to check the oil level rather than come in with me – a decision which mysteriously coincided with the sudden onset of a snuffly cold.

'Shall we go and see what they're up to?' said the proud new owner. 'I'm sure you'd like to see them before you go.'

Actually, I would rather have gone to the dentist, but to have bolted for the door would have seemed ungracious. We walked through into a sunlit lounge and there, sprawled out on the sofa, were Posh Paws and Ben. Posh Paws managed to open one eye as I stroked her silky head, but Ben snored through the emotional farewell with his usual fortitude in the face of adversity.

I knew my friends had found their forever home and would be far happier than they would ever have been with me. It didn't stop me snivelling all the way home, of course, but they were happy snivels – even if they did make me look like a particularly messy pumpkin.

AND FINALLY…

I hope you have enjoyed meeting some of the wonderful cats that have graced and continue to grace our lives. All cats – indeed all animals – are special, but there is something particularly rewarding when an animal that is down on its luck comes into your life and brings something new and wonderful into it.

Cats have brought huge amounts of love and humour into my life, not to mention some challenging moments, bless them! I even got a job once simply because my "interview skirt" was covered in fur and the person interviewing me was a cat lover, so forget about the Masonic handshake – in the right company, a few lumps of fur will open doors.

As for the wonderful friends I've made through rescuing and re-homing cats, I can only say that they have enriched my life beyond measure. There are a few people that I may have been less than pleasant to as I left with a traumatised cat or kitten; I hope I managed to shake their equilibrium with my parting speech because that was certainly my intention.

We must be brave, those of us who love animals, because we are often all that stands between them and the most appalling misery and suffering. It is a bonus that they never fail to repay us in so many wonderful ways.